ABC

ZooBorns!

Andrew Bleiman * Chris Eastland

BEACH LANE BOOKS
New York * London * Toronto * Sydney * New Delhi

T0024640

For my lovely wife, Lillian—A. B.

For Eloise and Lander—C. E.

Special thanks to the photographers and institutions that made *ABC ZooBorns!* possible:

Anteater:
Meghan Murphy/Smithsonian National Zoological Park

Baboon:
Marcus Birkenfeld, taken at Hagenbeck Zoo

Cheetah:
Meghan Murphy/Smithsonian National Zoological Park

Dhole:
Bobby-Jo Clow/Taronga Zoo

Elephant (page 10):
Brendan Johnson/New Mexico BioPark Society

Elephant (page 37):
Raymond Watt, taken at Rio Grande Zoo

Flamingo (page 11):
Richard Rokes/Riverbanks Zoo and Garden

Flamingo (page 37):
Ron Brasington/Riverbanks Zoo and Garden

Giraffe:
Patrick Bolger, taken at Dublin Zoo

Hippopotamus:
Bert Hulselmans/ZOO Antwerp

Impala:
Dave Parkinson/Tampa's Lowry Park Zoo

Jaguar:
Emmanuel Keller, taken at Bratislava Zoo

Koala:
Dreamworld, Koala Country Photographics

Lion:
Emmanuel Keller, taken at Zurich Zoo

Marmoset:
Wei-Hang Chua, taken at Alma Park Zoo

Nyala:
Stephanie Adams/Houston Zoo

Otter:
Sheri Horiszny, taken at Santa Barbara Zoo

Panda:
Jeroen Jacobs, taken at Chengdu Research Base of Panda Breeding

Quail:
Twycross Zoo

Rhinoceros:
David Mattner/Monarto Zoo

Sloth:
Amelia Beamish/Rosamond Gifford Zoo

Tapir:
Chris Humphries, taken at Linton Zoo

Ural owl:
James Godwin/ZSL

Vicuña:
George Griffiths, taken at Chester Zoo

Wombat:
Lorinda Taylor, taken at Taronga Zoo

X-ray tetra:
Brenna Hernandez/Shedd Aquarium

Yak:
Joachim S. Müller, taken at Bergtierpark Erlenbach

Zebra:
Blackpool Zoo

BEACH LANE BOOKS * An imprint of Simon & Schuster Children's Publishing Division * 1230 Avenue of the Americas, New York, New York 10020 * Copyright © 2012 by Zooborns LLC * All rights reserved, including the right of reproduction in whole or in part in any form. * BEACH LANE BOOKS is a trademark of Simon & Schuster, Inc. * For information about special discounts for bulk purchases, please contact Simon & Schuster Special Sales at 1-866-506-1949 or business @simonandschuster.com. * The Simon & Schuster Speakers Bureau can bring authors to your live event. For more information or to book an event, contact the Simon & Schuster Speakers Bureau at 1-866-248-3049 or visit our website at www.simonspeakers.com. * Also available in a Beach Lane Books hardcover edition * Book design by Lauren Rille * The text for this book is set in Century Schoolbook. * Manufactured in China * 0522 SCP * First Beach Lane Books paperback edition August 2015 * 10 9 8 7 6 * The Library of Congress has cataloged the hardcover edition as follows: Bleiman, Andrew. * ABC zooborns / Andrew Bleiman, Chris Eastland.—1st ed. * p. cm.—(ZooBorns) * Summary: "Calling all animal enthusiasts! It's time to scamper through the alphabet with a herd of irresistible zoo babies. Featuring adorable animal photos, a zippy text, and a fact-filled glossary, this just might be the cutest ABC book ever to hit the shelves!"—Provided by publisher. * ISBN 978-1-4424-4371-6 (hardback) * ISBN 978-1-4814-4703-4 (pbk) * ISBN 978-1-4424-4373-0 (eBook) * 1. Zoo animals—Infancy—Juvenile literature. 2. English language—Alphabet—Juvenile fiction. I. Eastland, Chris. II. Title. * QL77.5.B538 2012 * 591.3'92073—dc23 * 2011044439

The baby animals in this book want to help you learn your ABCs!

But that's not all . . . these cute and cuddly newborn zoo critters have another very important job. By allowing us to observe and study them, they help us learn how to protect their wild cousins who live in jungles, deserts, mountains, and oceans around the world.

The more you know about animals, the more you too can help protect them. So come on in and meet the ZooBorns. Then visit your local accredited zoo or aquarium to learn more!

Paul Boyle, Ph.D.
Senior Vice President for Conservation and Education
Association of Zoos and Aquariums

The Association of Zoos and Aquariums sets high standards to make sure all the animals at accredited zoos and aquariums get the very best care.

A

is for anteater.

I slurp up snacks with my extra-long tongue. Anyone for ants? Yum!

B

is for baboon.

Bananas are the best— and this one's all mine!

 **is for cheetah.**

You found my secret hiding place. *Shhh*, don't tell anyone!

D

is for dhole.

Don't you wish your peepers
were as dreamy as mine?

E is for elephant.

We elephants love playing ball. Heads up—it's my turn to kick!

 **F** is for flamingo.

My fluffy gray feathers will soon turn pink, just like my papa's.

G

is for giraffe.

I may be six feet tall, but next to Mom
I'm still tiny. (For now, that is . . .)

H

is for hippopotamus.

Calling all water babies—
it's playtime in my pool!

I

is for impala.

Our long legs are perfect for leaping. Let's go for a run!

J

is for jaguar.

I'm on the prowl for some grub.
Is it dinnertime?

 **K** is for koala.

I was born to cuddle. Mom's furry hug is just so snug.

is for lion.

Soooo sleepy… eyes droopy…
love my furry crash pad.

M is for marmoset.

Please don't tell anyone I'm monkeying around with my food!

N is for nyala.

Sometimes I nuzzle
Mama when I feel shy.

O

is for otter.

**We otter boys are sneaky.
Better watch out—
we might sneak up on *you*!**

P **is for panda.**

Phew... I'm flat-out pooped from playing with my panda pals.

Q

is for quail.

Even at my puffiest,
I'm still quite petite.

R is for rhinoceros.

We wrinkly rhinos are on the move. Follow us to the local watering hole!

 **is for sloth.**

Yawwwwwwn.

Is it siesta time yet?

is for tapir.

Well, hello there. I *thought*
I smelled something sweet.

U

is for Ural owl.

I wonder what's for dinner.
Mice would be nice!

V

is for vicuña.

Mama loves sniffing and smooching my silky-soft fur.

W  is for wombat.

After a big day of digging,
I'm all tuckered out.

X

is for X-ray tetra.

Attention, science students—my
see-through body is *very* revealing.

 **is for yak.**

Time for me to kick up my heels and hightail it home. See y'all later!

is for...

ZOOB

ORNS!

Get to know the ZooBorns!

Conservation Status Key

Critically Endangered: Extremely high risk of extinction in the immediate future

Endangered: Very high risk of extinction in the near future

Vulnerable: High risk of extinction in the near future

Near Threatened: May face threat of extinction in the near future

Least Concern: No immediate threat to the survival of the species

Species: Anteater (Giant)
Home: Smithsonian National Zoological Park, Washington D.C.
Conservation Status: Vulnerable
Little Pablo the anteater got off to a rocky start in life when keepers found him separated from his mother just hours after birth. Luckily, the pup is now doing well. Giant anteaters are the largest species of anteater. They have no teeth, but can slurp up as many as 30,000 insects in just one day!

Species: Baboon (Hamadryas)
Home: Hagenbeck Zoo, Germany
Conservation Status: Least Concern
Hamadryas baboons prefer life on the ground to life in the trees. Living in troops of 5 to 250 individuals, these social monkeys have a complex society in which one bossy male typically calls the shots. Hamadryas baboons were considered sacred by the ancient Egyptians.

Species: Cheetah
Home: Smithsonian Conservation Biology Institute, Virginia
Conservation Status: Vulnerable
Cheetah litters usually consist of many cubs, but when only one cub is born the mom does not produce enough milk to provide for her baby. This cub was an only child, so Smithsonian veterinarians matched two single cubs together with one mom, Zazi, who successfully fed and nurtured both of them. Cheetahs are the world's fastest land animal, reaching speeds of almost 75 miles per hour!

Species: Dhole
Home: Taronga Zoo, Australia
Conservation Status: Endangered
Jangala the dhole pup had to be hand-raised by keepers at Taronga Zoo but was eventually reintroduced to the adult group of dholes. Soon Jangala became so comfortable in the group, he took the dominant male position from his own father! Unlike most wild-dog species, dholes allow their pups to eat first at mealtime.

Species: Elephant (Asian)
Home: Rio Grande Zoo, New Mexico
Conservation Status: Endangered
Daizy was 318 pounds at birth, a healthy weight for an Asian elephant calf. The largest land animals in Asia, these elephants often come into conflict with farmers when they raid plantations looking for a tasty meal. Highly intelligent, Asian elephants have been observed making and using tools, just like humans and great apes.

Species: Flamingo (American)
Home: Riverbanks Zoo and Garden, South Carolina
Conservation Status: Least Concern
Flamingo babies begin life with gray feathers, which turn pink as the chicks begin eating tiny beta-carotene-rich shrimp and other crustaceans. In the wild, the American flamingo ranges from South America to the Caribbean, and occasionally finds its way to southern Florida.

Species: Giraffe (Rothschild)
Home: Dublin Zoo, Ireland
Conservation Status: Endangered
Giraffes have a fifteen-month gestation period, and their moms give birth while standing up. This means giraffe babies fall 6 feet to the ground when they're born! Standing 6 feet tall at birth, this newborn was a normal height for a healthy baby giraffe. He joins mother, Hailey; father, Robin; and sister Kuliko along with five other giraffes in the Dublin Zoo's herd.

Species: Hippopotamus
Home: ZOO Antwerp, Belgium
Conservation Status: Vulnerable
This playful youngster loves to frolic underwater, delighting ZOO Antwerp visitors. The third largest land animal, hippopotamuses spend most of their time semi-submerged, and their name actually means "river horse" in ancient Greek. However, despite its resemblance to

hoofed mammals, this species is actually most closely related to whales and dolphins!

Species: Impala
Home: Tampa's Lowry Park Zoo, Florida
Conservation Status: Least Concern
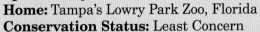
Impalas are outstanding jumpers, leaping distances of 33 feet in a single bound. They can also reach sprinting speeds of more than 50 miles per hour. With 2 million impalas ranging across central and southern Africa, they are among the most numerous species of antelope.

Species: Jaguar
Home: Bratislava Zoo, Slovakia
Conservation Status: Near Threatened
Born as part of the European Association of Zoos and Aquaria jaguar breeding program, this cub was one of two in mother Laima's first litter. Jaguar cubs are completely helpless when they're born, and Laima has proven to be a dedicated mother, providing excellent care and protecting her babies. Jaguars are one of only two big cat species found in the Americas.

Species: Koala
Home: Dreamworld, Australia
Conservation Status: Least Concern

Pound the koala is the poster child for a campaign to raise awareness of the challenges faced by koalas on the South Queensland coast of Australia. Koalas are marsupials, and they have a gestation period of only 35 days. Newborn koalas climb into their mothers' pouches, where they spend another 6 months growing and developing until they're ready to meet the world.

Species: Lion (Asiatic)
Home: Zurich Zoo, Switzerland
Conservation Status: Endangered

Once ranging from Italy and Greece through India and Iran, today the Asiatic lion population is mostly confined to the small Gir National Park & Wildlife Sanctuary in India. Urgent efforts are underway to protect the few hundred wild lions remaining, including involving local villagers in conservation projects. Zooborn lions like Jeevana offer hope for the survival of this rare cat.

Species: Marmoset (Common)
Home: Alma Park Zoo, Australia
Conservation Status: Least Concern

Native to the northeastern coast of Brazil, this adaptable little South American monkey has since found its way to southeastern Brazil, where it has actually become quite a nuisance to native species. Common marmosets feast on tree sap, but their nimble build also makes them experts at catching another favorite snack: insects.

Species: Nyala
Home: Houston Zoo, Texas
Conservation Status: Least Concern

The nyala is a shy antelope species that rarely ventures out of thick cover except to drink water. Nyalas are native to the dense forests of Southern Africa, where they live alone or in small herds of up to 10 individuals. Male nyalas are known for their beautiful spiraled horns.

Species: Otter (Asian Small-Clawed)
Home: Santa Barbara Zoo, California
Conservation Status: Vulnerable

This litter of 6 Asian small-clawed otter pups was the first of the species born at the Santa Barbara Zoo in more than 20 years! The pups stay close to their parents and spend a lot of time huddling together in the den. However, they also periodically emerge to take swimming lessons in shallow water with their parents. In the wild, this species is threatened by habitat loss, hunting, and pollution.

Species: Panda (Giant)
Home: Chengdu Research Base of Giant Panda Breeding, China
Conservation Status: Endangered

Giant pandas are born quite helpless, with their eyes closed and no fur or teeth. They live with their mothers until they are almost 2 years old. Though pandas are beloved around the world, this species faces huge conservation challenges. An exceptionally low birthrate combined with habitat destruction and poaching means that increasing the panda population is a slow, gradual effort. The total wild giant panda population is estimated at between 1,000 and 3,000 individuals.

Species: Quail (King)
Home: Twycross Zoo, United Kingdom
Conservation Status: Least Concern

This tiny chick and the rest of the babies in his clutch were raised with the aid of a heat lamp. The chick's mom mysteriously ignored her first clutch of eggs, leaving the zoo's bird keeper no choice but to incubate her eggs artificially. The tiny chicks were carefully monitored until they grew big enough to look after themselves.

Species: Rhinoceros (Southern White)
Home: Monarto Zoo, Australia
Conservation Status: Near Threatened

Packing on an average of 6.6 pounds every day, Digger the rhinoceros won't stay little for long! For the first few weeks of Digger's life, his mom, Umqali, sternly eyed both other rhinos and zookeepers, reminding them to stay away from her precious calf. Southern white rhinos are native to southern Africa, where they face poaching for their horns despite their protected status.

Species: Sloth (Hoffman's Two-Toed)
Home: Rosamond Gifford Zoo, New York
Conservation Status: Least Concern

Born underweight, Ruth the sloth bounced back thanks to keepers who supplemented her mom's milk with nutritious formula. Now Ruth is happy, healthy, and as active as a sloth ought to be, which is to say, pretty laid-back. Sloths are not endangered, but deforestation in Central and South America means their habitat continues to shrink.

Species: Tapir (Brazilian)
Home: Linton Zoo, United Kingdom
Conservation Status: Vulnerable

Born as part of the European Breeding Programme, this little calf was baby number 11 for tapir parents Shannon and Tanya. A Brazilian tapir calf's stripes provide natural camouflage against predators in the wild. Generally shy creatures, tapirs are known to dive into the water when alarmed and use their flexible snout as a snorkel.

Species: Ural Owl
Home: ZSL London Zoo, United Kingdom
Conservation Status: Least Concern

The Ural owl's range extends from Europe to northern Asia, but no matter what country it calls home, it always looks for a cozy hole in a tree to build its nest. Ural owls aggressively defend their nests when they have chicks. They've even been known to chase away humans!

Species: Vicuña
Home: Chester Zoo, United Kingdom
Conservation Status: Least Concern

Vicuñas live in high-altitude areas of the Andes Mountains in South America. This beautiful creature is the national animal of Peru. While wild vicuña populations today are estimated at over 350,000, it was not always this way. In the 1970s wild vicuña populations had fallen to only 6,000 individuals. Luckily, conservation efforts helped the population rebound in a big way. Vicuña fur is prized for its softness and in Incan society it could be worn only by royalty!

Species: Wombat (Common)
Home: Taronga Zoo, Australia
Conservation Status: Least Concern

Orphan wombat Mirrhi required round-the-clock care when she was brought into Taronga Zoo's Wildlife Hospital, but she is now doing great. Wombats like Mirrhi are built for digging, with big teeth and powerful paws. These specialized marsupials even have a backward-facing pouch, so dirt doesn't get inside when they are burrowing!

Species: X-Ray Tetra
Home: Shedd Aquarium, Illinois
Conservation Status: Not Classified

True to its name, the X-ray tetra has a largely transparent body, making it a great teaching tool for fish anatomy! This species eats small insects and plankton and lives in coastal rivers in South America.

Species: Yak
Home: Bergtierpark Erlenbach, Germany
Conservation Status: Vulnerable

Shaggy-coated cousins of the cow and buffalo, yaks are among the largest of all bovines. Once numerous across the stark Tibetan plateau, wild yaks are now rare due to overhunting. Domestic yak dung is still valued as a fuel source for cooking fires and for warming travelers in remote areas of Tibet.